Self-Esteem

A Self-Help Book Filled With Effective Techniques To Enhance Your Confidence And Self-esteem, Providing Immediate Empowerment And A Positive Emotional Experience

(A Path To Self-Relationship, Increasing Self-Value, And Managing Your Emotions)

Josef Balzer

TABLE OF CONTENT

Get Some Confident Habits 1

The Cycle Of Life: Accepting That Everything Changes, Even Sentiments. 5

Energy Efficiency: Optimizing Peak Operating Durations 22

How Can I Become More Self-Compassionate? 40

Set Goals And Manage Your Time Prudently 53

Methods For Mastering And Managing Depression 63

What Are The Expectations? An Outline 109

Level Up Your Confidence 123

Get Some Confident Habits

Changing your behaviour on the outside is one method to alter how you feel on the inside. Losing self-worth and confidence frequently leaves you feeling unmotivated to accomplish anything worthwhile. Along with this, you surround yourself with comforting objects and food. This comfort quickly becomes a habit, and habits are hard to quit.

You hear the advice to "get exercise and eat healthy" a lot. This is one of the best strategies to regain confidence because feeling better physically will lift your spirits. The same holds for having a restful night's sleep. You feel better on the inside when you get enough sleep, making you feel better overall.

Positive self-talk will be another habit of confidence. When you speak poorly of yourself, you give a bad impression to everyone around you. However, you will see significant improvements if you develop the habit of speaking positively.

Consider Your Previous Accomplishments

It's time to take a moment to reflect on your past experiences and achievements. You may persuade yourself, "Look at what I've done before, I can be just as great or even better than that," when you witness their accomplishments.

One thing you may do is compile a list of your greatest to-date accomplishments. A strong grade, a seat on the squad, or even troubleshooting a technological problem at home can all count. Everything that has proven useful ought to be on the list. You can use this list to refute any doubts about your abilities whenever they arise. A notebook, or notebooks, is an excellent instrument for monitoring this. You'll want to keep track of a lot of stuff, so I would advise getting a couple.

You may see things for what they truly are when you incorporate mindfulness into your daily life. It's the best defence against these internal conflicts. Therefore, I wholeheartedly recommend being more aware of both the outside world and oneself.

Establish Objectives You Know Will Boost Confidence

We will discuss this in more detail later in the book, but when you establish objectives for yourself, choose ones that you are confident you will achieve. Creating a "step system" of smaller objectives that build towards your main goal is the most effective method to set them.

You are giving yourself more accomplishments to look back on in the future when you set smaller goals. Therefore, you are increasing your confidence now and in the future. Once more, we will discuss goal-setting, vision boards, and related topics later on.

*****

It is the one inside of you that aims to make you feel good about yourself and raise your self-esteem, but if you put in the necessary effort, you can prevail in this struggle. My one warning here is that things will come in the way, and it can appear quite simple to revert to behaviours that foster poor self-esteem. Treat yourself kindly on your journey, and refuse to see your missteps as failures. These are opportunities for learning, nothing more.

The Cycle Of Life: Accepting That Everything Changes, Even Sentiments.

To overcome unrequited love, the person must face the truth of life's cycles and the cyclical nature of emotions. Chapter fourteen will discuss the significance of acknowledging that feelings and emotions are subject to change. Acknowledging the transient nature of emotions can offer a person a more expansive and freeing viewpoint to progress toward emotional recovery.

The unceasing stream of feelings

Emotions are a natural and ever-changing aspect of the human experience. Emotions, like ocean tides, come and go, evolve, and alter over time. Understanding that the emotional suffering experienced after heartbreak is subject to change requires accepting its dynamic nature.

Understanding that emotions are fleeting

It might be difficult to accept that emotions pass, particularly while experiencing the sorrow and anguish of a broken heart. But it's crucial to remember that no emotion lasts forever and that the severity of the suffering will ultimately subside.

The relationship between feelings and ideas

Emotions and thoughts are intimately related. Emotions can affect thoughts and vice versa. Recognizing this link might assist the person in challenging harmful thought habits that can be causing them ongoing emotional suffering.

Acknowledging ambivalence in emotions

It's common to feel conflicted about love when trying to move past unrequited love. The person may experience various emotions simultaneously, including hopelessness, rage, grief, and despair. Letting emotions come and go on their terms requires first accepting this emotional ambivalence.

The influence of radical acceptance

Embracing radical acceptance is letting emotions come and go without opposition or criticism. Releasing the person from internal conflict and promoting a better self-awareness can be accomplished by acknowledging that emotional suffering is inevitable in getting over heartbreak.

The value of being in the moment

One technique to cope with the unpredictability of future emotions is to bring your attention to the here and now. Feeling grounded and more connected to oneself can be achieved by living in the present and being conscious of the emotions being felt at that very moment.

Gaining the ability to let go

To let feelings come and go on their own, one must learn to let go of expectations and emotional ties. Letting go is about releasing the emotional hold that heartbreak can have on a person's life, not about forgetting.

establishing a loving connection with oneself

One step in developing a loving relationship with yourself is acknowledging that feelings fluctuate.

The person can develop a closer, more loving relationship with their inner self by realizing that self-love is a necessary component of emotional recovery.

Emotional self- care's echo

Taking care of oneself emotionally allows you to respect how emotions change over time. Self-care activities like writing, painting, exercise, and meditation can help the person let go of negative feelings and express them constructively.

The efficacy of patience and time

Time is a helpful ally when trying to move past heartache. The key to emotional healing is giving yourself the time and space to allow feelings to shift and heal.

The significance of getting assistance

specialists for emotional support when you're coming to terms with the fact that everything changes, including your feelings. Talking to others about the event can be consoling and offer an unbiased viewpoint, making it easier to view the circumstances from several perspectives.

The reflection of individual development

Accepting that everything is subject to change can be a process of emotional and personal development. Resilience and flexibility can be enhanced by learning to go with the flow when experiencing emotional ups and downs.

The Emotional Heartbeat in Conclusion

To embrace the fundamental essence of existence is to accept that everything changes, even sentiments. Emotions are like a never-ending emotional heartbeat;

they come and go in response to events and situations in life.

The knowledge that their emotional suffering is transitory and that, like ocean tides, sentiments eventually find equilibrium and change might console the affected person.

In this chapter, the individual learns to welcome feelings' shifting nature and allow them to flow without opposition or judgment. It is an act of self-love and compassion to accept that everything changes. This lets life carry on, bringing fresh chances, opportunities for personal development, and a revitalized sense of optimism for the future.

4.3 Promoting Physical, Mental, and Emotional Health

However, ADHD has a significant impact on mental health in addition to its obvious consequences on day-to-day employment.

According to neuroscience, the complex interaction between the limbic system—which controls emotions—and the prefrontal cortex may impact the link between emotional well-being and ADHD. A study found that people with ADHD may have more powerful emotional reactions and struggle to control their emotions.

Comprehending this intricate interplay is crucial in formulating all-encompassing therapies for ADHD that tackle the cognitive and affective dimensions of the illness. People with ADHD may be able to comprehend and manage these interactions.

For ADHD, Self-Care Is Essential People

To thrive while dealing with ADHD, self-care is crucial. Living a happier and more balanced life begins with realizing the importance of self-care. Self-care is a crucial tactic for preserving mental health because people with ADHD frequently deal with certain difficulties that could have an impact on their emotional health.

Living with ADHD involves managing symptoms that can impair a variety of daily functioning, including time management, organization, impulse control, and emotional regulation. Up to 70% of people with ADHD suffer from emotional dysregulation, according to Healthline.

The difficulties these symptoms present must be recognized to appreciate the necessity of self-care. Acknowledging the necessity of self-care enables individuals to adopt proactive steps towards preserving their health and accept individualized solutions.

Why Is It Important to Maintain Emotional Health?

We know that emotional wellbeing is a prerequisite for overall mental health. When people with ADHD put their emotional wellbeing first, they may experience improved emotional regulation.

reduced stress and increased ability to bounce back from setbacks

Self-care techniques that improve emotional well-being, such as mindfulness training, deep breathing exercises, and fun hobbies, can lessen the highs and lows that come with ADHD.

How to Take Care of Yourself Practically as an Adult with ADHD

Living with ADHD might present challenges in engaging in effective self-care. You may establish a helpful atmosphere and acquire the skills necessary to thrive with ADHD by customizing your self-care routines to meet your needs. Here are some useful tactics to think about:

Creating a Customized Schedule and Program

Someone with ADHD may benefit from having a sense of regularity and order by creating a customized timetable and strategy.

Create a daily schedule that allows specific time for:

Balance Between Work and Life Work out Relax

Set reasonable deadlines and attainable objectives to promote a full and enjoyable day. See which scheduling methods work best for you by experimenting with different approaches, such as time-blocking strategies, calendars, and apps (some of our top picks are included below).

Including Techniques for Mindfulness and Meditation

Practices in mindfulness and meditation can help you become more adept at controlling your emotions and maintaining focus. Develop a present-moment awareness through deep breathing, mindfulness practices, or meditation to potentially offset impulsive and distraction.

Additionally, mindfulness meditation may ease stress, promote relaxation, and improve cognitive performance. To promote mental clarity and emotional well-being, consider incorporating these techniques into your daily routine.

Are you prepared to live in proportion, harmony, and balance?

Learn more about our Essential Mindfulness Course, designed to improve your overall well-being and executive functioning. Come on in right now.

Utilizing Tools and Resources to Control Stress

For those who have ADHD, stress management is essential because it can aggravate symptoms. Investigate stress-reduction strategies like journaling, progressive muscle relaxation, or a new hobby.

Effectively managing stress may also help you keep your emotional equilibrium and improve your focus.

The Advantages of Exercise for Symptoms of ADHD

Regular exercise has several advantages for ADHD sufferers. Concentration lessens anxiety and depressive symptoms.

Include enjoyable workouts, such as yoga, dance, or brisk walks, in your regimen. Regular exercise enhances your physical and mental health, general well-being, and cognitive performance.

Increasing Sleep Quality to Promote Mental Health

Getting enough sleep is crucial for enhancing mental wellbeing and lowering ADHD symptoms.

Establish a regular sleep regimen.

Establish a relaxing evening ritual.

Improve your sleeping space to achieve restorative sleep.

Limit your screen time before bed.

To promote a calm transition into sleep, think about relaxing activities like reading or listening to music. A consistent sleep schedule can improve mood, focus, and overall cognitive performance.

Getting Assistance and Guidance from Professionals

While managing ADHD, there's no reason to be afraid to seek expert assistance. A qualified psychologist, coach, or counsellor can provide people with specific coping mechanisms, methods, and skills to help them deal with life's obstacles.

Therapy aids in emotional healing, increases self-awareness, and improves comprehension of your ADHD. Successful self-care routines and improve your emotional well-being.

4.4% Managing ADHD to Achieve Success

It's critical to keep in mind that it does not characterize you. You may thrive and make the most of your special abilities in addition to managing your ADHD symptoms with the correct techniques, attitude, and support.

Acknowledging ADD

ADHD is a feature of how your brain processes information; it is not a limitation. Acknowledge this distinction. It frequently coexists with inventiveness, intense concentration, and skilful multitasking.

Seek Expert Advice

Consult a medical professional first. They might assist you in creating a personalized treatment plan that calls for medication, counselling, or lifestyle modifications.

It's Important to Have Order

To keep organized, spend money on tools like planners, to-do lists, and digital applications. Creating routines and dividing the effort into smaller, more doable activities could be helpful.

Meditation and mindfulness

You may decrease your impulsivity and increase your attention span by practising mindfulness and meditation. You may be able to exert more control over your thoughts and behaviour by employing these approaches.

Energy Efficiency: Optimizing Peak Operating Durations

Energy Efficiency: Optimizing Peak Operating Durations

First of all,

controlling your energy is equally important as controlling your time to achieve maximum performance and lasting productivity. The conventional focus on time management is frequently ignored. Key energy management components are optimizing your activities at peak performance and knowing your body's natural rhythms. This extensive book will review the fundamentals of energy management, methods for locating and optimizing periods of optimum performance, and the advantages of matching your work to your energy levels.

1. The Constant Productivity Fallacy

The Obstacle:

A widespread misunderstanding is that productivity can be sustained and continuous throughout the day.

The Resolution:

Identifying Energy Valleys and Peaks: Recognize and accept the cyclical nature of energy. Throughout the day, your body goes through high and low energy phases. Identifying and honouring these cycles is the foundation of efficient energy use.

- Quality Over Quantity: - Put quality production instead of continuous output as the main emphasis. Working more efficiently when your energy and concentration are at their highest is more important than working longer hours.

2. The Energy Peaks and Circadian Rhythm

The Challenge: Ignorance about the body's intrinsic clock can lead to mismatched task planning.

The Resolution:

Comprehending the Circadian Rhythms: The circadian rhythm spans a 24-hour period and is the body's internal clock that controls numerous physiological functions. Get to know your circadian cycle to recognize the peaks and valleys of your natural vitality.

- Normal Energy Maximums:

- Energy seems to peak in the late morning (about 10 AM) and early afternoon (around 2 PM) for many people. Schedule intense, creative, and problem-solving work during peak productivity.

3. Assessment of One's Own Energy

The Problem: People might not completely understand their unique energy patterns.

The Resolution:

- Performing an Energy Assessment on Oneself: - Maintain a journal to monitor your concentration and energy levels throughout the day. When do you feel most awake, focused, and able to handle challenging tasks? This assessment will assist you in determining your energy peaks.

How to Spot Energy Drains: Determine which activities also deplete your energy. It might be specific chores, meetings, or outside circumstances. Reduce the amount of energy these activities use or plan for times when you have less energy.

4. Aligning Assignments with Energy Levels

The Challenge: Inefficient work might result from misaligning tasks and energy levels.

The Resolution:

- Strategic Task Scheduling: - Match work to available energy. Set aside periods of high energy for jobs that need strategic thinking, creativity, and problem-solving. Put off mundane or administrative work until you have less energy.

- Batching Similar Tasks: - Consolidate related tasks into a single energy block. This preserves your mental energy by reducing the cognitive strain of continuously switching between different kinds of activity.

5. Breaks' Power

The Problem: Skipping breaks can lead to burnout and decreased productivity in general.

The Resolution:

- Strategic Breaks: - Plan out your day with strategic pauses. You may stay focused and replenish your energy by taking a little rest. Schedule breaks during lower-energy periods to avoid pushing through weariness.

- Microbursts of Movement: During breaks, employ microbursts of movement. Engaging in short-term physical activity can increase your energy levels. To revitalize your body and mind, try taking a quick stroll, stretching, or practising deep breathing.

6. The Significance of Diet and Hydration

The Obstacle:

Dehydration and poor diet can have a major effect on energy levels.

The Resolution:

- Balanced Diet: - Provide your body with meals and snacks that are in balance. Steer clear of hefty, energy-draining foods that can make you feel lethargic. Choose a diet high in proteins, healthy fats, and complex carbohydrates to maintain energy.

Drink plenty of water throughout the day. Fatigue and a decline in cognitive function can be caused by dehydration. Try to drink water regularly and keep a bottle at your desk.

Last Thought: Building Unwavering Self-Esteem

This voyage of self-discovery and personal development has concluded. In this book, we'll look at the core principles of self-worth and how to develop it firmly throughout your life. In this last section, I want to underline the significance of applying the most important lessons we discovered and summarise them.

The Self-Esteem Journey:

You are constantly on a mission to achieve unwavering self-esteem. We begin by appreciating the significance of our self-image and how our beliefs and self-compassion influence how we see ourselves. We develop strong self-esteem that is unaffected by the opinions of others as we learn to deal with criticism and judgment from the outside world.

Assertive Communication and Emotional Resilience: We examine emotional resilience as a strategy for overcoming obstacles and life's transitions. Adaptability has become an asset that helps us advance even in the face of difficulty. We discovered that assertive communication is essential to wholesome relationships and effectively communicates our wants and perspectives, asserting Rejection and Failure: We accept that rejection and failure do not determine our value. Rather, we observed how these circumstances may fortify us and impart important knowledge.

Professional Success and Self-Improvement: We understand that the secret to professional success is self-improvement. By investing in our personal growth, we increase our self-assurance and ability to handle obstacles at work.

Day Celebration: We have finally realized how important it is to commemorate our trip. Acknowledging our successes, no matter how minor, makes us stronger and inspires us to continue our quest for unwavering self-worth.

Your Self-Esteem's Future:

Remember that your self-awareness and personal development path is far from finished when you put this book away. Maintain a strong sense of self-worth, act authentically, and focus on developing emotional resilience.

In your daily life, apply your lessons here as guidance. When you do, you'll be ready to take on obstacles with assurance, form deep connections, and lead a happy life.

Thank you for sharing this journey with me. I hope your self-worth keeps growing, illuminating your way to a promising future.

Though it is the end, this is also a fresh start. Proceed with confidence and self-worth, for you deserve all that life has to offer.

How did you find the book?

To my dear reader,

First, I want to express my gratitude for spending the time reading this book. My earnest goal is that you have gained insight and motivation to develop unwavering self-worth in your life.

Your review and comments are very valuable to me as the author and to other readers who might be thinking about picking up this book. Not only may your words assist me in my future job, but they can also help guide and influence the decisions of others.

How to Give a Book a Kindle Rating on Amazon:

I'll walk you through the easy process of rating a book on Amazon Kindle. Here's how to do it:

First, visit the book page by logging into your account on the Amazon website.

- To locate the book you read, enter the title or my name as the author in the search bar.

- To view a book's page, click on its cover.

Step 2: Scroll to Customer Reviews - Locate the "Customer Reviews" section by swiping the book page.

Step 3: Click "Write a customer review." A "Write a customer review" button is directly underneath the customer reviews. Press the button.

Step 4: Compose Your Review – You have reached the review composition section. Your rating of the book can range from 1 to 5 stars. The greatest rating possible, five stars, denotes a truly positive experience with the book.

- Write your review after that. You can discuss the book's positive aspects, personal benefits, and any other ideas you'd like to share with other readers.

Step 5: Submit Your Review - After submitting your review, click the "Submit review" button to share it.

And prepared! We will be grateful that you shared your review, which other readers will see.

Please remember that your review can give me, the author, invaluable input while also assisting others in making well-informed decisions about reading this book. Your viewpoint is essential.

Once again, I appreciate you reading this book and considering writing a review.

Your involvement is necessary for this endeavour to be successful.

CHAPTER 4 4.1: Getting Rid of Limiting Thoughts

The path to creating riches starts in the mind, a place that is sometimes obscured by constrictive ideas that impede development. This chapter begins with breaking down the barriers of self-doubt and discussing the importance of rephrasing our ideas. By using the experiences of individuals who have overcome their obstacles as a source of inspiration, we shed light on the importance of self-awareness and its capacity to awaken the latent potential within each of us. "Cultivating a Wealth Mindset" serves as a helpful reminder that belief is the foundation upon which wealth is constructed.

Three Steps to Develop a Wealth Mindset and Get Rid of Limiting Beliefs

First Step: Recognize Limiting Beliefs

Start by becoming aware of the self-limiting ideas that you hold.

Think about the ideas that make you feel insecure or impede your efforts to build riches. The first step in breaking free from these self-doubt bonds is awareness.

Step 2: Challenge and Reframe

Reframe your beliefs by deliberately working to identify them. Present proof that refutes pessimistic beliefs to counter them. Look for instances of people who overcame comparable obstacles and succeeded. You start to weaken the foundations of self-doubt by changing your viewpoint.

Promote Self-Awareness in Step Three

Develop self-awareness as a compass. Evaluate your feelings, ideas, and responses regularly. Recognize and change limiting thoughts as they come up. You can awaken the latent potential within yourself by accepting self-awareness and realizing that belief is the foundation of your riches quest.

CHAPTER 4 4.2: Developing Calm Inner Conversation

Self-talk is the quiet builder of our reality, operating within the chapters of our story. The art of cultivating positive self-talk—a practice that tends to the seeds of self-worth, self-confidence, and resolve—is explored in the second section. We discover that the words we say to ourselves become the guiding lights that show us the way to financial success through stories that highlight the transformational power of self-affirmation. "Cultivating a Wealth

Mindset" pushes us to develop a garden of empowering self-dialogue, where doubt withers and opportunity blooms flourish.

Three Steps to Developing a Wealthy Mindset via Positive Self-Talk Step1: Awareness of Your Talk

Start by developing a keen awareness of your dialogue. Be mindful of the internal conversation that occurs in your head. Determine any negative, self-critical, or self-doubting tendencies. This increased consciousness creates the conditions for change.

Step 2: Use Affirmation in Place of Negativity. Actively substitute empowering self-statements for your negative self-talk. Use affirmations that will empower you to counter any self-limiting beliefs you may be having. Make a list of affirmations that speak to your values and aspirations. Regularly repeat these affirmations to bring positivity into your inner dialogue.

Step 3: Apply Uniformity

Consistency is essential to cultivate constructive self-talk. Include empowering ideas and affirmations in your everyday activities. Include them in your journaling sessions, morning routines, or quiet times for thought. This technique will gradually change how you talk to yourself, creating a garden of resilience, self-assurance, and willpower that will point you toward financial success.

How Can I Become More Self-Compassionate?

I got to where I am now by using self-discipline and self-compassion. It helped me understand how to move forward in addition to getting me through a divorce.

It's okay if I am constantly failing at things! It indicates that I'm developing, learning, and moving forward. It's acceptable to experience discomfort when trying new things, and boy, did I try some new stuff! At times, the learning curve was so steep that I would not have survived without my sense of self-worth, compassion, and self-control. It would have felt like the falls were too harsh and the mountain was too high.

How can you increase your self-compassion to become the best version of yourself? A lot of it will depend on your unique situation. Here are some suggestions to get you going!

Determine WHY you behave the way you do toward yourself!

If you want to increase your level of self-compassion, start here. We spoke about how different circumstances can make it difficult for people to practice self-compassion in chapter 5. It might have cultural roots. It might have something to do with trauma in the family. It might be brought on by loneliness or a deeply held belief.

Consider the following questions to help you identify the root cause of your lack of self-compassion: Why do I treat myself this way?

Why can't I prioritize my time, sleep, mental wellness, and health?

Why does standing up for my principles and limits hurt in this situation?

I learned how to treat myself this way: from who or what?

What fear makes me treat myself worse in this circumstance than I would someone I love?

Identifying the factors that drive your current self-compassion—or lack thereof—will help you determine the most effective techniques and approaches.

For example, if you disregard therapy to address an abusive relationship that created your inner critic, writing and mediation may not yield much benefit.

If you are unwilling to question the notion that you must be hard on yourself to succeed, therapy will not work.

If you do not create boundaries with individuals in your network who believe self-compassion is selfish and lazy, trying to prioritize yourself will be an uphill battle.

When you discover the WHY, you'll be able to identify what needs to come first to successfully increase your self-compassion. If necessary, seek the advice of a trained therapist, a sympathetic friend, or a comforting relative to talk things through and hear their points of view.

Say Yes When Those Around You Say No.

Being hard on oneself because of cultural or familial expectations can make it difficult to exercise self-compassion. But it's crucial to remember that self-compassion is a basic human need that may be developed independently of one's upbringing, community, or cultural background. Despite what the outside world may say, an individual can practice self-compassion in the following ways:

★Become knowledgeable: It's crucial to grasp the advantages of self-compassion and the fact that it's a basic human need. It will help you discover the drive to strive to be kinder to yourself when the rest of your world is suggesting differently.

★ Begin modestly: At first, engaging in self-compassion practices may feel awkward or even incorrect. It's acceptable to begin modestly by thinking good thoughts for oneself or indulging in something tiny.

★Locate a community: Connecting people attempting to develop self-compassion can be beneficial through workshops or online support groups. Through your library or community centre, you may also be able to identify others in your neighbourhood who would be interested in starting a coffee meet or compassionate group stroll.

★Employ imagery: Self-compassion exercises can be done with the help of visualization. For instance, they could put themselves in the shoes of a tiny child and provide comfort and kindness to that child. Consider what you would say to a close friend or relative in the same circumstance. What would a caring and compassionate person in your circle say to you? These visualization exercises facilitate visualizing the experience of taking a more compassionate stance.

★Have patience: Becoming self-compassionate takes time and practice, especially if it defies cultural expectations. It's critical to practice self-compassion. Don't be hard on yourself for not being an expert at it. Accept it as evidence that you are improving and learning.

It's crucial to remember that altering the habits and ideas you have always followed is a difficult and gradual process. Even when everyone disapproves of your plan, you may still develop self-compassion by starting small and being patient with yourself.

Get Past Your Scars

Having gone through a difficult upbringing or traumatic event can make it difficult to have compassion for oneself. But it's crucial to keep in mind that developing self-compassion is a skill that can be learned. Following a challenging event, you can practice self-compassion by following these steps:

➢ Seek support: Consulting with a therapist or counsellor can be beneficial in helping you process the trauma and dispel any misconceptions you may have formed as a result of the incident.

➤ Take care of yourself: Taking part in activities that enhance one's mental, physical, and emotional health can support self-compassion development. Exercise and engage in enjoyable activities regularly.

➤ Use mindfulness techniques: Much of the day is spent in autopilot, with little to no thought given to what we do or why we do it. Feelings while stepping back from. The negative things you say to yourself and the timing of those statements.

➤ Identify and replace your negative self-talk with messages that are kinder and more compassionate in order to challenge negative self-talk. You may rephrase your inner critic's comments,

"I'm such an idiot," for instance, to something like, "It's okay to make mistakes, I'm doing my best."

Retell your narrative from the perspective of a survivor rather than a victim, and acknowledge the grit and resiliency you have displayed in the face of hardship.

➤ Exercise forgiving others: You don't have to forgive them for them to hurt you again or for them to get back in. To heal, it is necessary to let go of the hurt. Additionally, work on forgiving yourself for previous transgressions or feeling powerless in the face of tragedy. Additional advice can be found in the following guidelines and Chapter 3's self-esteem-building advice.

Remember that becoming a self-compassionate person takes time and practice after a traumatic event. It's critical to practice self-compassion and ask for help when needed.

Decide to cultivate a culture in which you never give up on your objectives in the face of unanticipated obstacles and delays. Your goals should never be thrown aside. When you are worn out, you can take a nap to rejuvenate yourself before getting back up to resume your admirable race. Recall that persevering for your objectives is a courageous act of not giving up on what you truly want and not giving up on yourself. It is an act of love and self-compassion.

Every day, schedule time unhindered for the things you enjoy and are passionate about: Your choices determine the course and appearance of your days. You must choose to enjoy yourself and do what you love without reservation. If you are bored with your daily activities, life is trying to remind you that it's time to actively fulfil your desire for a joyful and exciting life. While pursuing your objectives and finishing your daily tasks is admirable, failing to take care of your happiness can lead to self-inflicted unnecessary agony and boredom. You could be shocked by how much you will love it if you dare to try new things and investigate what makes you happy with an open mind!

Exercise Every Day

Every day, teens go through a wide range of emotions on an emotional roller coaster. Remembering that this is normal and a necessary aspect of your humanity is critical. Emotional processing is a skill that must be developed on your own; nobody is born with it. Suppressed emotions impact you and everyone around you when they are improperly processed. Your emotional intelligence has the potential to either build or impair your relationships. I will push you to make it a habit to purposefully set aside time each day to analyze your feelings and determine the best course of action for you. You can discover entertaining and inventive ways to spend these 15 or 30 minutes each day. Consider the various locations you might go to take some time to reflect on yourself and refresh your soul. By practising self-care, you'll be able to show up more every day for yourself and your relationships and avoid spending your days feeling lost and frustrated.

Which lesson did you take away from this chapter the most? This chapter's main goal is to make you understand that you must always love yourself more than anyone else can and always be relentlessly compassionate toward yourself. Everyone encounters difficulties and makes mistakes occasionally; there's no need to punish yourself or deny yourself the chance to move on. Where there is negativity, choose to disengage and instead plant encouragement and seeds of compassion, love, and positivity. This is

---

an effective formula for building a lovely and contented life.

Set Goals And Manage Your Time Prudently

I can still clearly recall seeing how different people's unique production habits depend on whether they set goals. A day spent with defined goals in place produces entirely different outcomes than one spent with none at all. Your productivity soars when you have well-defined objectives and remain committed to achieving them. You risk losing out on possibilities for advancement when you begin each day without a clear sense of purpose or direction. You soon find yourself putting all your energy into whatever grabs your attention, even if it means you're not getting closer to realizing your goals. When someone needs greater discipline to set objectives and work toward achieving them, time is lost and wasted. On the other hand, when you set goals and take the necessary steps to achieve them, you can innovate and accomplish a limitless amount in a single day.

I unfortunately waste every day I don't with them through whatever obstacles. Every day, I set clear objectives and work hard to get them, which I will always be proud of. Making the most of your time each day and organizing your days will lead to a good life. Speaking, wishing, and daydreaming about everything you want to do is great, but your ambitions will remain unfulfilled without thoughtful, well-thought-out action.

Time well set realistic objectives for yourself and develop sound financial habits even as a teenager.

Why, in your opinion, is time management and goal-setting always such a major deal? Have you ever wondered what a difference it will make to not establish daily goals and just go with the flow of each day? It's important to think about how important goal-setting is. Establishing goals and pursuing them with tenacity is a habit and culture that will greatly assist you in drawing in far more success than you could have imagined. Being lazy and complacent is easier than putting in the effort and doing what needs to be done. Living without feeling pressured to complete tasks by a certain deadline is more pleasant and enjoyable. You may avoid stagnation and stay in your comfort zone by defining goals and being deliberate about reaching them. You'll never be able to completely appreciate your potential without plans. Most people's lives are shaped by their objectives and aspirations when they are young or adolescents. The most important period to seek advice and instruction on action plans to make your ambitions come true is adolescence. A dream is an idealized picture of what you would like to achieve. For that vision to become a reality, having well-defined objectives and a solid action plan would be ideal. Your objectives then serve as the roadmap for achieving your aspirations. While certain goals can be accomplished every day, most tasks require time. Whether your dreams come true or remain unfulfilled depends on how you spend your time.

Which dreams do you have? Make a list of the top five things you would like to do. Next, ask yourself what you must do to fulfil your dreams. Others won't exploit you to achieve their goals if you know what you value and want. Has the adage "whoever doesn't invest in building their plans will be hired to make other people's dreams" ever occurred to you? This is a very important life lesson. Setting goals will enable you to make the most of your time. You have probably had days when you've wondered what precisely you did to make the day worthwhile. You might have been depressed over your day's lack of productivity. On other days, you've made an effort to be productive so that you can feel good about yourself at the end of the day.

The following bullet points provide clear explanations of goal-setting best practices, the importance of objectives, and possible viewpoints:

Setting goals enables you to communicate your values and identity: The world is eager to see what talents and gifts you have to offer to improve it. More than any spoken description of your identity, the objectives you set and how you work toward them will reveal more about who you are. Your ideas, mindset, and attitude are all reflected in your dreams. They reveal your identity to everyone, including you. Reaching your objectives will help you gain the respect of people and silence your detractors.

Growth, not perfection, should always be the main priority: It feels fantastic to fully reach your goals. However, it's acceptable if the model isn't always feasible. If you shift your understanding of embodiment, you can stop being so hard on yourself when things don't turn out exactly as you had hoped. For instance, you may have a very clear idea of the grades you hope to receive during your final exam in school. You may become upset if the results are not exactly what you were expecting when they are ultimately announced. When things like this occur, it's normal to feel unhappy; nevertheless, it's not acceptable to believe that you are a failure and to blame yourself for the simple reason that things did not go as planned. Cherish the experience and all the personal development you gained along the way. Progress, not perfection in and of itself, defines a meaningful and fruitful existence.

Develop your ability to quickly adjust and be adaptable when necessary: Goal-oriented Teens tend to perform well, but there is a drawback if they don't allow flexibility when needed. Setting goals forces you to concentrate your time, energy, and attention on particular tasks. As you reach your objectives, chances to carry out unanticipated ideas generally present themselves. This can limit your ability to advance and become competent if you cannot concurrently figure out a method to prevent losing out on unanticipated possibilities. Never giving up on your objectives is a terrific habit, but it's even more amazing if you can teach yourself to adjust fast to changes and add more plans as time goes on. Always have an open mind when it comes to your aspirations. Your desires vary as you develop and learn new things. If you adjust to your evolving vision, you can take advantage of additional opportunities outside of your initial goals.

Reward and celebrate yourself for every objective you've done. Occasionally, you might think celebrating your hard work is only appropriate if you've reached your goals. But that's just treating yourself harshly and ridiculous. Reaching objectives can take a very long period. Would you like to spend months denying yourself joy and festivities?

Divide your goals into manageable daily tasks, and remember to treat yourself when you meet them. Additionally, it will revitalize and inspire you, giving you more energy to pursue the remaining goals.

When establishing your goals, there are four things you should consider to help you stay on course and get ready to tackle any roadblocks that may arise. These are the following:

Vision: What result and kind of reality are you hoping to achieve? How does it appear? How may realizing this vision benefit me? What does it mean to me to achieve my goals?

Process: What approach are you going to take to reach your objective? How do you intend to achieve your goals, and what strategy will you use?

Restrictive elements: You have to enumerate every possible hindrance and difficulty. What may cause an issue to arise?

A counteractive action plan comprises the techniques and tactics you can use to handle any issues and constraints.

Following the above basic criteria, you can help yourself develop quantifiable, time-bound, and realistic goals.

Methods For Mastering And Managing Depression

All of us previously had aspirations and dreams of the things that would make us happy—things we wanted to be or do. Somehow, as we grew older and life's stresses and anxieties began to consume us, we lost sight of our dreams, and for some of us, the battle with depression became more pressing.

Being patient and allowing oneself time to recover is essential to conquering depression. It is vital to realize that it is possible. Yes, climbing that hill may require significant time, work, and support, but once you do, things gradually begin to feel much better.

A Day at a Time There isn't a miracle treatment or recipe that can instantly lift your depression. Taking each day as it comes is the greatest way to begin your recovery. Avoid trying to take on too much at once. Remind yourself that certain things require time and give yourself a break. Remember to take each day as it comes; if you don't succeed today, there's always tomorrow.

Find a Reason to Fight - Even when you feel like giving up. We can only move forward one step at a time; therefore, keep moving forward. This stage will be easier for you if you have a target or something to strive for. It is necessary to have a dream to strive for. Giving up on all of your aspirations shouldn't be the response to depression. It implies that while achieving them can take a little longer if you are persistent, you can succeed. You may find that your dreams are what motivate you to continue.

Remember That It's Not Forever Every Day - Sad moments will pass. Remember that this storm will pass whenever you feel like drowning in sadness. This darkness won't endure forever when you keep pushing daily to see the light again.

Locate ONE thing for which you are thankful every day. Every morning, as you wake up, think about one item for which you are thankful. For the remainder of the day, use this as your anchor. If your thoughts are taking over, go back to your cause for gratitude today and focus on it until you feel better.

As a reminder that even in the depths of your despair, there is always something in your life for which you are thankful, tell yourself your reason several times during the day. Family, for instance.

Or the affection of a dependable spouse.Anything that motivates you to carry on. Concentrate on one at first, and progressively increase it as you begin to feel better.

The Painful (Literally) Consequences of Negativity

If you're wondering if bad feelings affect your health, the answer is yes. It's called "powerful" for a reason, and since negative emotions have already been directly connected to several health-related issues, they are particularly harmful. These heightened levels of cortisol and adrenaline coursing through our veins are known as "stress hormones," they give us the energy to respond forcefully and quickly. Frequent emotional upheaval can result in stress; as we all know, stress is bad for the body.

Among the most common reasons for migraines and headaches is mental stress. The next time you experience a severe headache or migraine, note whether you were under any stress before the headache started. This phenomenon can arise because, in a stressful scenario, the brain releases chemicals that may create alterations in blood vessels, which in turn causes a headache. Anxiety and worry, two extremely stressful emotions, cause us to tense up our muscles more, which widens blood vessels and exacerbates headaches and migraines.

Your headaches and/or migraines are either recurrent or intermittent. The latter typically occurs in the event of an exceptionally stressful circumstance. On the other hand, it can result from a tension build-up that intensifies and finally materializes as your headache. Because episodic headaches occur occasionally, over-the-counter medications are a simple way to treat them. In this situation, practising relaxation techniques and avoiding stressful triggers also help.

The course of treatment for chronic headaches is a little more involved. Depending on the severity of your illness, antidepressants, counselling, stress management classes, and maybe medication to reduce anxiety are all feasible options. Certain individuals' hormonal alterations during a stressful episode, according to some scientists, are sufficient to cause a migraine to start. A variety of factors may cause your migraine, but one thing is certain: these triggers are nearly invariably unpleasant and unfavourable circumstances or experiences.

Taking Control of Your Guilt and Fear

Codependents often experience strong feelings such as guilt and dread when they consider saying "no." These feelings may be difficult to control when defining limits and expressing wants. A crucial stage in the codependency treatment process is getting over these emotions. This is how one could face and overcome fear and guilt:

1. Acknowledgment of the Right to Say "No": It's important to recognize that everyone can voice their demands and set boundaries. Saying "yes" to every request or demand is not required.

2. Examining the Sources of Guilt and Dredity: It's important to investigate the causes of guilt or dread as they become apparent. Are they the result of expectations and pressures from the outside world, or are they based on one's ideas and values?

3. Redeployment of Negative Thoughts: Rejecting negative ideas and engaging in introspection related to saying "no" is critical. Positive, empowering ideas take the place of these unfavourable perceptions. "I am a repugnant person for declining" is replaced with "I am taking care of my well-being by setting this boundary."

4. Self-Compassion Practice: It is recommended that one treat oneself with kindness and compassion. It is our responsibility to understand that saying "no" is an act of self-care rather than selfishness.

5. Emotional Regulation Proficiency: The ability to control emotions, particularly guilt and anxiety, is developed. Progressive muscular relaxation, awareness, and deep breathing support this ability.

6. Incremental Exposure: It is advised for those whose fear of saying "no" hangs over them to gradually expose themselves to scenarios that call for boundary assertion. Starting with less difficult cases is a useful strategy.

Practical Step: Role-Playing Scenarios Involving "No"

Engaging in the following practice scenarios with a friend or therapist can help one become more comfortable saying "no" and strengthen assertiveness skills:

1. Rejecting a Social Invitation: Practice politely and assertively turning down a social event or invitation in a role-playing environment.

2. Enforcing Work limits: Learn how to express your desire for a work-life balance and draw limits in the workplace.

3. Dealing with Manipulative Requests: Put yourself in scenarios where someone tries to guilt-trip or coerce you into saying "yes." Gain the ability to react to these situations with confidence.

Expression of Personal Wants: With the help of a friend or therapist, engage in a role-playing exercise to discuss your wants and expectations in a relationship or a particular situation.

5. Handling Unwelcome advice: Think through and practice saying "no" when someone tries to give you unwanted advice or interferes without permission. At the same time, be respectful and firm.

Saying "no" is a talent that develops and improves with practice. As one becomes more skilled at making themselves

3.3 Pay Attention Actively

"By being truly interested in other people in two months, you can make more friends than you can in two years trying to get people interested in you." Carnegie Dale: Almost any aspect of your life can be improved by effective communication. Effective communication abilities will benefit your personal and professional connections and help you succeed in business. All of your relationships may experience a variety of issues as a result of poor communication. It's a skill that can tremendously affect practically every part of your life.

Although listening might not immediately come to mind as a crucial aspect of communication, it is. All calls have half of them listening. To be an excellent communicator, one must be able to listen with honesty.

Active Listening: What Is It?

As one might anticipate, active listening is paying attention to what the other person is saying. It just refers to listening intently to the person speaking to you. This is not the same as the often-seen passive listening in conversations.

When you listen to someone actively, you use your senses. It also entails giving the guy your undivided attention. It's important to demonstrate to the other person that you genuinely listen to them; your body language will convey this to them.

Imagine that your body demonstrates that you are fully present in the moment and engaged in what is being said while your brain actively listens and understands. It's the ideal method for visualizing helpful listening.

The Value of Paying Attention

Before delving into the specifics of active listening techniques, let's examine the significance of active listening.

You will undoubtedly understand that listening is a crucial component of communication if you think having effective communication skills will improve your connections. That concludes our discussion.

Whenever feasible, it is highly recommended to engage in active listening for the following reasons:

Fosters Mutual Confidence

Someone will instantly think you care about what they have to say if they observe you actively listening to them. It's common knowledge that most people enjoy understanding others very much. It's one of those things that genuinely lifts our spirits.

Someone can't help but believe that you're attempting to understand them when you are genuinely interested in what they say. This essentially greatly impacts how much they think they can trust you.

Increase Self-Belief

Active listeners seem to have more self-esteem and a better sense of who they are. They are masters at creating and preserving strong, dependable bonds. People who continuously act this way seem confident in their abilities.

Reduced Errors and Miscommunication

You're probably taking in a ton of subtleties and details that you would have missed otherwise if you weren't practising active listening. You're only listening with half an ear if all you're doing is waiting for someone to finish talking so you can speak. Additionally, doing so ensures that flames will miss certain crucial points.

If you pay attention to what someone else is saying, you might notice many small details and nuances.

Enhanced Output

Consider being given a job assignment. Now, picture the individual who assigned you the work explicitly outlining every step of the assignment from start to finish. Now, picture that individual paying attention to your responses and asking any questions you may have.

You leave the conference with a clear idea of what you want to accomplish and how you will do it. That's a nice feeling, isn't it?

Finding someone who can speak well and listen to you without judgment will greatly impact how well you complete the project. You have an easy-to-follow route map to get where you're going.

Lessening of Arguments

Recall that feeling understood is one of the greatest joys for every one of us. That's pretty crucial in this case.

One of the primary causes of the ongoing intensity of disputes is a lack of understanding. We feel much more thorough if someone is listening to us. Therefore, when we feel heard, we trust the other person more and choose not to quarrel. Finding a workable answer is far simpler for everyone.

Openness Levels

The term "active listening" is a bit misleading. You seem to be merely shaking your head while occasionally asking questions while sitting there. That's not how it works. Think of a continuum as a line that extends from the left (cold) to the right (warm). A closed individual, located at the coldest point on the continuum to the left, willfully chooses not to communicate with you out of fear, ambivalence, or dislike. Open people are on the extreme right of the spectrum; they are at ease, trust in you, and regard you with great respect. They also freely share with you their thoughts, worries, and dreams. Your goal is to move in the spectrum, right? Move your chat companion from cold to dry to open. The drawback is that you can't stay silent; you must be almost as transparent as they are. If they feel comfortable sharing a story from their early years, you should be, too. You can't expect them to go much further if you don't. Most likely, they don't. It is an exceedingly essential concept— starting from closed to open collaboratively. It also connects to the two broad strategies for opening up to others:

You can try to move your companion to a more comfortable spot by pinging them. As an illustration, you could pose an open-ended question like "How do you think you'd feel if that happened to you?" that goes a little bit further than they've shown thus far. In the next section, we will talk about making assumptions, another significant type of pinging.

Alternatively, you can take the lead by deciding on the level of transparency you want your partner to be at and offering to go there first. That doesn't have to be a significant change. Telling a coworker a nice childhood story could be one way to gauge their level of openness.

In real terms, this implies that even while actively listening, you are still speaking quite a bit. Talking to them just serves to rouse them. Pinging explicitly invites them to participate, and Going First can require you to give lengthy, drawn-out anecdotes. The idea is that you're learning more and more about them and connecting everything back to them. You'll know you've accomplished when they engage with the topic rather than providing a canned response. Just watch out that you don't ping too hard. It's not safe to inquire about memories of a traumatized childhood if you are thinking about the weather. Go First in small stages, and remember that it is rare for negative subjects to be okay. Even in exceptional situations, you won't discuss your sadness or therapist with your closest friend or relative. People occasionally simply don't feel comfortable with you delving deeper. That's acceptable. Remember that this is an easy time for them, and try again later. It takes an extra twenty minutes, it takes an extra twenty years, or it's the subject.

Simply stay put once you've advanced to a new level. Now that Jenny has expressed her thoughts about Nepal, I will ask her about her empathy and wonder how it influences her decisions in life. This is very important to me. It's possible that we won't even discuss my water tale, which is fortunate for me because I don't want to think about it. I had never before read the story. Of course, you must climb the ladder, but at least now you know how to do it deliberately. Try it out, and then give it another rinse.

So, what is the process here? How do we change our reality and bring about favourable circumstances? Being conscious is the first step. We must become conscious of the energy we project into the universe and our ideas and feelings. We might begin to recognize any unfavourable habits or limiting thoughts preventing our aspirations from materializing by being aware of our interior condition.

We can reorient our thoughts and emotions toward the frequencies corresponding with our aspirations as soon as we become aware. Practice and deliberate effort are needed for this. It entails rewiring our minds, substituting uplifting ideas for pessimistic ones, and developing an attitude of thankfulness and plenty.

Visualization is a useful tactic to bring about favourable circumstances. We can draw the life we want into our reality by clearly visualizing it. The subconscious mind, the engine of manifestation, is triggered by visualization. The universe responds to our unambiguous signals about what we want by bringing it into our experiences when we picture our desires regularly.

Affirmations are an additional tactic. We may retrain our subconscious minds to believe that we can manifest our dreams by repeatedly saying good things about ourselves and our goals. Affirmations support a mental shift from uncertainty and anxiety to trust and confidence. They serve as profound reminders of our actual potential and the boundless possibilities in the cosmos.

Another essential component of creating favourable conditions is gratitude. Sincere appreciation for what we already have allows us to be receptive to more. Our gratitude shifts our attention from scarcity to plenty and from fear to love. It opens us up to receiving and makes it easier for the universe to give us what we want.

Ultimately, manifestation requires inspired action. Merely seeing, affirming, and expressing thankfulness is insufficient. We also need to act in a way that advances our objectives. This entails following our passions, paying attention to our instincts, and having faith in the universe's direction. By acting in a way that fulfils our desires, we let the universe know we're prepared to get what we've been asking for.

By using these doable tactics in our everyday lives, we can begin to attract favourable events and change the course of events. There is no slow approach to applying the Law of Universal Attraction. It necessitates engagement and a dedication to our development. We become co-creators of our reality, moulding our experience and releasing the magic within us as we tune into the appropriate frequencies, match our thoughts and emotions with our desires, and take inspired action.

Considering the Inner Power

As we get to the end of this chapter, pause to consider the profound truth we have all discovered. The secret to bringing the enchantment back into our lives is to connect our thoughts and emotions with the frequencies that draw the things we most want by applying the Law of Universal Attraction. Using this ability, we may also build a successful, joyful, and loving reality.

Throughout this chapter, we have discussed the fundamentals of the Law of Universal Attraction and how it affects our lives. We've seen how our feelings and thoughts operate like magnets, drawing good and bad things into our lives. We have explored the ideas of vibration and energy and how they influence our reality. Additionally, we know how to change our lives and attract favourable circumstances through doable tactics.

However, why is any of this relevant? Why should we spend time, energy, and focus learning about and using this fundamental law? The secret is in the limitless potential waiting to be discovered within us. This book is about awakening the cosmos within ourselves, not just about acquiring abstract concepts.

We are starting a path of self-exploration, development, and metamorphosis by accepting the Law of Universal Attraction. We accept responsibility for our ideas, feelings, and deeds and realize we can design the life we want. Although this path is not always simple, it is very fulfilling.

Imagine living a life where you are excited and have a purpose every morning when you get up. Where you effortlessly draw opportunity, wealth, and deep connections. Where challenges become stepping stones to your personal and professional success, this life awaits those who dive deep into learning the Law of Universal Attraction and master its precepts.

I, therefore, warmly welcome you to join me on this life-changing adventure. Give up on any doubts or scepticism that might be preventing you. Embrace the power within you, and trust in the workings of the cosmos. We will spark our desires, connect with the energy around us, and create a reality that aligns with our authentic selves.

We will delve into deep ideas, useful activities, and motivational tales in the upcoming chapters, all of which will help you along this path of awakening. We will probe deep into your being, revealing unspoken convictions and rewiring your brain for achievement. Remember that the universe is always there to help you and that you can change your life.

Friend, are you prepared? Breathe deeply, sense the energy surrounding you, and let's go on this journey together. Prepare yourself for an experience that will make you aware of the universe within you as we reveal the keys to regaining prosperity, happiness, and love.

And never forget that you are the one with power. Always has, and always will.

3.4. Dangers of Inadequate Timing-Missed Opportunities: Moving too slowly could lead to missed opportunities while moving too quickly could result in missed details or benefits.

-Eroded Trust: Trust may be damaged if quick timing is interpreted as pressure tactics or delays are considered stalling strategies.

-Reduced Leverage: While waiting too long may appear stubborn, making concessions too soon might lessen negotiation strength.

3.5. Differing Cultural Timing

Understand that views of time are influenced by cultural variations. For example, in certain cultures, developing a relationship comes before conducting business, while in others, making choices quickly and on time is crucial.

Timing is the beat and the rhythm of the complex ballet that is negotiation. It raises the performance, directs steps, and orchestrates movements. Negotiators can successfully negotiate the dance by comprehending, honouring, and effectively using timing. Ultimately, the composition of a successful negotiation is not solely determined by what is said or done but also by when it is said or done.

4. Dealing with Impasses and Arguments

Regardless of experience level, every negotiator will encounter deadlocks—moments when neither side is ready to give ground, and the chance of a successful resolution appears remote. Disagreements and deadlocks are inevitable in the negotiation process but are not insurmountable barriers. Rather, they are obstacles that may become chances for more in-depth comprehension and cooperative problem-solving if handled with care, patience, and strategy. This section breaks down these difficult times and provides advice on how to deal with them.

4.1. Identifying the Causes of Blockages

Understanding the cause of a deadlock is essential before taking any action. Typical reasons include:

-Mismatched Expectations: Different goals or outcomes envisioned by each party.

-Cultural or Communication Barriers: Misunderstandings brought on by variations in expressions, language, or cultural standards.

-Emotional Factors: Past grievances, mistrust, or personal animosities impacting the negotiation.

- Information Asymmetry: Parties owning varying levels or quality of information.

4.2. Preventive Steps to Reduce Conflicts

Often, prevention is preferable to treatment:

- Clear Agendas: Having well-defined goals and agendas for talks helps direct the discourse and reduce side topics.

- Developing Rapport: Spending time fostering relationships can reduce tense situations.

- Transparent Communication: Misunderstandings are less likely when both sides have access to crucial information.

4.3. Methods for Ending Deadlocks

- Take a Break: Even a brief distance might provide new insights and lessen intense emotions.

-Reframe the Discussion: Move the conversation away from divisive topics by taking a different tack or bringing up fresh ideas.

-Seek Common Ground: Restate agreed goals or principles to foster a cooperative environment.

-Explain the Third Party: An unbiased advisor or mediator can close gaps, promote dialogue, and provide new perspectives.

-Prioritize subjects: To establish momentum and trust, divide the discussion into smaller segments and start with the less difficult subjects.

4.4. Handling Emotional Conflicts

When conflicts stem from feelings or prior encounters:

- Active Listening: Even if you disagree, ensure the other person feels heard and understood.

- Empathize: Acknowledge and affirm their emotions while exhibiting sincere comprehension.

-Express regret if required: If you were part of the mistrust or complaint through previous acts, own up to it and extend your apology.

-Aim to Reestablish Trust: Consider behaviours that foster trust, such as keeping your word and communicating openly.

4.5. Recognizing When to Leave

Sometimes, it can be appropriate to put the negotiation on hold or end it altogether:

-Pre-established Boundaries: Establish your "walk-away" points—conditions or results you are unwilling to accept—before starting negotiations.

- Balance the Pros and Cons: If the possible benefits are no longer worth the time, money, or effort, consider taking a step back.

-Keep the Door Ajar: Even if you decide to leave, ensure it's a cordial parting that leaves the door open for possible future conversations.

While difficult, impasses and arguments can be incubators for development, comprehension, and creativity. They test the negotiator's abilities, endurance, and flexibility. Nevertheless, these deadlocks can become cooperative bridges with the appropriate tactics. Negotiators may create agreements resonant with wisdom, respect for one another, and shared success by viewing conflicts as riddles that need to be solved rather than as immovable obstacles.

Section 8: Penalties

Each person needs discipline to maintain control over their lives. It inspires someone to succeed and move on with their lives. Everybody is in charge of something in their lives. Furthermore, everyone has a different definition of discipline. While some consider it a significant aspect of their lives, others do not. Availability is the road map that points one in the correct direction.

A person's life will be dull and meaningless without discipline. Furthermore, a dedicated person can manage and navigate life more advancedly than a non-dedicated person.

You also need attention if you have a plan and want to see it through to completion. It will help you succeed and make things easier to handle in the long term.

There are typically two different types of discipline when discussing them. Self-discipline and enforced discipline are the two types of discipline.

We either pick up discipline from other individuals or from observing other people. Conversely, we have to learn self-discipline on our own. It is difficult to practice self-discipline without much support and motivation from others.

Above all, maintaining perfect adherence to your daily schedule is another aspect of being focused.

The rationale behind your demand for strictness

In life, almost everything demands concentration. Therefore, it's advisable to begin practising discipline as soon as feasible. Self-discipline is defined differently by each individual. For a youngster, a worker, and a student, it implies something different.

Furthermore, what discipline means might vary depending on the occasion and context. Gaining discipline is difficult since it requires a lot of effort and patience. It also requires a sound body and a contented mind. One needs to be extremely disciplined to be effective. The Benefits of Discipline

The follower functions as a stairway to assist the person in reaching their destination. It assists someone in maintaining focus on their life objectives. It also prevents him or her from straying.

Additionally, it makes a person an ideal member of society by instructing and educating his body and mind to obey rules and regulations. This brings perfection to that person's existence.

The diligent individual has more opportunities than the undisciplined person at work. It also offers the individual a very distinct aspect of themselves. Furthermore, the individual always leaves a positive impression on others they encounter.

Ultimately, it is imperative to acknowledge the significance of discipline in every individual's life. To be great, a person must lead a disciplined, healthy, and regulated life. Additionally, discipline benefits us much and inspires seriousness in those around us. Above all, discipline enables individuals to reach their desired goals.

States of trance

enhanced internal focus, less awareness of the outside world, and enhanced receptivity to suggestion are characteristics of trance states, which are altered states of consciousness. In these states, the mind may be more receptive to behavioural and cognitive changes and is more focused on thoughts, sensations, and visions.

The procedures used, and the objectives of the individual desiring to enter a trance might determine the many forms and levels of trance states. These are some instances of hypnotic states.

Light trance: In this stage, the person's focus is more inward, but they are still conscious of their surroundings. This type of trance is frequently employed in relaxing meditation techniques and hypnosis induction.

Deep Trance State: During a deeper trance, the person may become more focused on their internal ideas, feelings, and pictures and less conscious of their surroundings. Hypnosis sessions or profound meditation exercises can help one reach this condition.

Autonomous trance state: In this condition, the person goes into a trance on their own, without the help of a therapist or other authority figure. For instance, when completely absorbed in a creative endeavour or passionate pursuit, some persons may enter trance states.

Flow trance: This mental condition happens when someone is totally engrossed in something, losing track of time and space. This is a state that musicians, artists, and sportsmen frequently go through when they are creating or performing.

Meditative trance state: This condition, attained by various meditation techniques, denotes increased focus and self-awareness. The person in a meditative trance may feel a profound sense of inner peace and connectedness.

Numerous goals can be achieved by inducing trance states, such as self-discovery, relaxation, improving performance, hypnosis therapy, and more. It's crucial to remember that trance states differ from person to person and are a normal aspect of the human experience. A well-trained professional's guidance and the appropriate usage of trance states can make them effective tools for mental and emotional health.

How affirmations can help you make great changes in your life

Our beliefs greatly influence our feelings, and optimistic thinking produces self-assured, content individuals. Negative thinking, on the other hand, results in low self-esteem and many missed opportunities in life. Having a positive outlook on life is crucial to happiness and success. We doubt ourselves much too often and put ourselves down far too frequently—all of which we do without even realizing it. Our minds are filled with hundreds of unpleasant thoughts every day. A person's negative thought patterns can be changed, and regular positive affirmations can greatly enhance their quality of life. This instrument can be utilized all day with very little effort on the user's behalf. They can enhance your life in various ways, such as increasing your self-knowledge and awareness and making you feel more confident, self-assured, and self-aware.

However, what precisely are these "positive affirmations"?

You will experience benefits in your life from utilizing positive affirmations, and the more you use them, the easier it will be for positive thoughts to replace negative ones. Throughout the day, you can employ positive affirmations wherever and whenever you need them. A straightforward strategy that may be used to change negative self-talk—which most of us engage in without even realizing it—into a more optimistic perspective on life is the usage of affirmations. It will take time to change our thinking and how we think because most of us have exposed ourselves to a constant stream of negative ideas for a considerable time. But once you've successfully retrained your thinking, you will start to notice effects if you stick with affirmations. These are some of the most popular and useful affirmation techniques for addressing different situations.

The mirror strategy

To develop self-worth, self-awareness, and self-esteem, you should stand in front of a mirror—ideally a full-length one—either in your underwear or, better yet, completely nude. This method helps you cultivate these attributes and learn to love who you are. You may say something like, as you work your way down your body, saying out loud what it is you like about different parts of your body. Say, As you cultivate a more positive self-image, take your time and move gently over your entire body. Saying something like, "My eyes are a fantastic attribute; they glitter and glint," would be an example.

The technique is portable.

Imagine turning down a volume dial within your skull so you can no longer hear unpleasant thoughts when you catch yourself thinking them. You can use this approach anytime you find yourself thinking something unpleasant. Consider yourself having a negative thought when you recognize that you are thinking one. The second step is to turn the volume back up while repeating the affirmation to yourself, replacing the negative idea with a good one.

The way a trash can is used

When negative thoughts arise, write them down on paper, roll them into a ball, and throw them in the trashcan. By doing this, you are telling yourself that these thoughts are worthless and that the trashcan is the appropriate location to dispose of them.

The meditation technique of sitting

Choose a quiet, tranquil area, close your eyes, and spend five to ten minutes letting go of all thoughts and emotions. Recite your affirmation aloud to yourself repeatedly, paying close attention to what you are saying and putting your faith in it. Spend a minimum of a few minutes doing this every day. Everything Is in Our Heads,

What Are The Expectations? An Outline

Have you ever observed those who seem at ease, composed, and self-assured and wondered whether they are mentally doing something different? What makes some people happy with who they are, while others work so hard to develop a different self-image that they think other people would find appealing?

Since 2014, I have been leading group training courses and one-on-one coaching sessions as a coach and trainer in emotional wellness. I've had the chance to spend hours hearing people's innermost thoughts and feelings—their problems, goals, and aspirations.

A few years back, I decided to gather the ideas and guiding principles of my clients who had achieved the outcomes they desired for themselves. Clients who struggled to pursue their objectives with total conviction shared another trait I discovered: they appeared to be more concerned with what other people thought of them than with what they desired. Whether they aspired to pursue their passions, find a partner they liked, or start a novel career, their fear of what other people would think of them outweighed their desire to make their ambitions come true.

My goal in producing this book is to provide a comprehensive guide for everyone who wants to attain their goals but is constrained by other people's ideas and judgment.

We are all the same somehow, even though we are all unique. Everyone wants to be accepted and liked. Within each of us lies a small child who fears rejection. Sometimes, our bigger life—one that enables us to embrace our actual selves and offers us the satisfaction of being the distinctive individuals we truly are—is thwarted by our fear of rejection.

This book will reveal to you:

The top 7 strategies for letting go of other people's opinions

How to confidently and unwaveringly pursue your dreams despite other people's opinions

How to handle divergent viewpoints without endangering your relationships

The methods we employ to read people's minds and how to mitigate the negative consequences

Why attempting to win people over really makes them dislike you

The main worry that causes us to worry about how other people perceive us and how to best handle it

Tried-and-true techniques for being yourself, completely and unashamedly, while automatically projecting a positive image of yourself.

The paradoxical rationale for why individuals attempt to exert control or influence over you

I've had the honour of travelling this path with my clients and seeing firsthand how improving themselves helps them succeed. These encounters have improved my understanding of people and the mental states that contribute to success. I am obligated by confidentially not to provide any personal information about my clients in this book. I have, however, tried to impart my observations of what has worked successfully for them using fictitious scenarios.

At the end of this book, you will be rid of the worry about what other people may think. I can't wait to tell you what I've noticed. So, let us get started right now.

Creating a Positive Attitude

It's critical that you mentally prepare for your journey toward better self-esteem. You have to use the power of your expectations to make it work. You must teach yourself to forget about the doubters and assume the journey will be beneficial. To enable you to move forward, let go of security, anxiety, criticism, past, family, partner, closest friend, doubts, inadequacies, and responsibilities.

Let rid of the negative and focus on just one thing at a time: imagine your life as it would be if you started to achieve your goals. How would you live? What could you accomplish for humanity and yourself? What level of intelligence would you contribute? How might this affect your sense of self-worth? Get rid of anything that is preventing you from answering that one question.

Few people make an effort to value their individuality. Not many people expect diversity. Though few individuals can accurately forecast happiness, you can overcome the odds and aim for the stars. Develop the mental habit of always viewing yourself and your objectives favourably.

You may be accustomed to focusing more on what you lack than what you do have. Grief may be taking up more of your time than happiness. You may focus more on your mistakes and failures than your journey's victories. You may be more fixated on discomfort than satisfaction. You could focus more on the confusion than the objective. Can you make out the pattern?

Focusing on your life's purpose and objectives will help you achieve what is genuinely yours. Establishing your objectives will be among the most fulfilling things you can do for yourself, even though it might not be easy. If you honestly examine your priorities, goals, and desires, you can identify your sense of purpose more readily. Think about why you're going through this difficult journey, what you want to achieve, how you want to get there, and who you want to be when you arrive.

Beliefs that are both realistic and constructive can help you along the way. When you have positive beliefs as a guide, they will help you get to where you need to go to move ahead with what you want to build. The same is true for your core beliefs. When your core beliefs are realistic, they will direct you to think realistically about your experiences, relationships, and yourself, allowing you to move in a positive direction. Your self-esteem grows along with these positive core beliefs.

Setting Realistic Goals

According to statistics, developing healthy self-esteem has practical, favourable outcomes when working toward definite, realistic goals. This is far more effective than simply repeating mantras and seeking approval from others.

A goal can be anything you want to own, become, or accomplish. Goals can be monetary, psychological, health-related, academic, or personal. They might be short-term to long-term goals. They might be as simple as cleaning your desk regularly or as complex as launching your business.

Goal setting seems simple because we always do it in our heads and even on a whim. But goal setting is a serious affair if you are passionate about improving unfavourable aspects of your life, striving for positive results, and developing healthier self-esteem. It's the blueprint that may take you places that only a few people ever imagine, much less explore.

One goal should not conflict with another. If you set a goal to spend more time playing with your younger sibling or helping your parents around the house and then set another goal to study as many hours as possible to get a better grade, you've made goals contradicting each other. Neither will be accomplished. This also means that a minor goal should not conflict with a major life goal.

For example, your primary life goal, propelling everything in your life, might be, "I will never deceive or hurt anyone else to get ahead."

However, if you set another goal that declares, "I will become the best student (or enter the best school, win the best award, win every race or competition) no matter what the cost," this goal would directly conflict with your ultimate life goal.

Goals should include an action verb. You shouldn't start a goal statement with wording like "I want to..." or "I intend to...." These are unattainable targets because they lack passion and drive! Begin with phrases like "I am going to..." or "I will..." Can you tell the difference between the two? The first two are undecided. However, the latter two examples are certain.

Goals also need completion dates. Without time constraints to reach your objective, there is no drive, urgency, or sense of motivation to achieve that goal. Without a deadline, you risk implying that you're not fully committed to your goal.

Finally, all goals must be signed by you, which we will go over in detail during Activity 5 later in this book. Your signature represents your dedication to the goal. It implies that you are making a personal commitment to yourself. It states that you want to strive toward this goal to achieve higher self-esteem.

Don't forget! An implementation plan must also accompany your goal. The implementation plan is sometimes referred to as targets. This is your goal's appetizer. This is the critical phase where you decide how to achieve your goal. How do you intend to save for your dream dress? Will you take on part-time work? Do you intend to open a bank account? Are you planning to cut back on other expenses? How do you intend to save this money? What is your strategy?

This is where you need to be as specific as possible. These steps must be practical and achievable for you. You might need to start easy and work your way up or take small, consistent steps toward your larger goal.

Let's assume your goal is to buy the dream dress you've been eyeing through the glass while window shopping without asking your parents for money. Your goal-setting plan to make the money can look like this:

I will figure out the exact price of the dress.

I will determine the amount of time I want to save money.

I will decide whether to save in a bank account or use a piggy bank.

I will find a way to save money, whether a part-time job or cutting expenses out of my allowance.

I will stick to my goal and save the money before the goal completion date.

Your goal might be different, but for everyone, there must be a plan for achieving it. Someone who sets frequent targets and reviews their progress regularly will be able to do more in a shorter amount of time and develop feelings of drive and focus. Setting a balance of short-term, medium-term, and long-term targets is also beneficial. Too many long-term goals might be disappointing and frustrating without short-term targets to inspire us.

Level Up Your Confidence

To gain a deeper understanding of self-esteem and its significance, we thoroughly explored its theories in Part I. We'll look at more of the doable actions we can take in this second section of 13 Steps to Optimum Self-Esteem to begin raising or lowering our self-esteem levels so we can reap the full advantages of being at our best. In the book's last chapters, we will continue to rejoice over all those advantages.

We began to realise that levels of self-worth are not fixed and that various triggers can negatively impact oneself. It's possible that something happened between now and last year, making your self-esteem feel much more brittle now than it did then.

Thus, understanding that self-confidence and self-esteem are not the same thing forms the basis of this section—learning the skills we need to ensure we can have robust, stable, healthy, and non-contingent levels of self-esteem.

Consider a well-known performer who can act or sing in front of millions of people on stage but who returns home at night to try to numb the agony of poor self-worth by engaging in risky and addictive behaviours that could even endanger their lives. This illustrates the difference between self-confidence and self-esteem. This person does not regard or love themselves, even though they have mastered their craft and can walk boldly on stage to all that attention!

When you consider that self-esteem is a "value" judgement you make about your "Real Self" and your essential worth, and self-confidence is mostly about self-trust, you will be able to appreciate the crucial distinction between the two. Thus, despite their self-confidence, our celebrity despises who they are. This indicates that while feeling more confident might boost our self-esteem, it should not be used as a replacement for self-esteem. Rather, it can be a component of the strategies we use to reach our highest level of self-esteem.

You might have come across my book due to concerns about your lack of confidence and discovered that poor self-esteem could be the root of the problem while researching ways to boost your confidence. It follows that even if they are different, you cannot correct one without fixing the other. Furthermore, self-doubt, the antithesis of self-confidence, may be counterproductive.

Let's examine self-confidence now and see how well we can do!

USE YOUR SELF-CONFIDENCE OR LOSE IT

Do you know the true cause of most people's failure to fulfil their potential? It has everything to do with their self-belief or lack thereof and has nothing to do with intelligence, opportunities, or resources. Put differently, your self-assurance can inspire you to pursue and achieve your goals.

It is easy to believe that having confidence is only a result of luck or genetics and that people who possess it were fortunate enough to be born with it, but that is untrue. Like skin or eyes, confidence is a trait that can never change; rather, it is the outcome of our thoughts and beliefs.

Here's an illustration. Let's say you want to work on a project with more value at work, but you feel stuck in an unfulfilling and dead-end career. What's holding you back? Is it a case of those positions you would prefer not to exist (which is unlikely), or is your inability to apply for the career of your dreams due to a lack of confidence? What do you think will occur if you attempt to switch careers? Have you convinced yourself that there are so many more qualified individuals that no one would ever give you a chance, or do you think you will find the ideal job and be able to convince a new employer that you are the ideal fit for that post with ease?

Our beliefs determine our actions, which also influence how we view ourselves. If we think we will fail, it will come to pass or, more likely, we will talk ourselves out of trying to spare ourselves the embarrassment of failing.

Chapter Four has shown us that we can rewire our minds and adopt new perspectives. Better yet, we can accomplish this at any age or stage of our lives, and one belief we can begin to alter is our sense of self-worth, which manifests as faith in our capacity for success!

The term "volitional" used by psychologists to describe this indicates that "it is a choice."

It is possible to increase your self-confidence, but it will require effort. Recall a period when you excelled at work or in school. Do you recall the sensation you had when you received many compliments? Your self-esteem surged and most likely remained quite high for some time, or at least until you were chastised for something else, experienced rejection in a romantic relationship, or felt ignored by loved ones.

I want you to think back on these emotions because they demonstrate that, similar to self-esteem, confidence may fluctuate. The good news is that this implies we have the power to intentionally make decisions that will boost our confidence. Imagine that your confidence is like a hidden muscle that has become flabby if you work out in any way, even if you don't go to the gym.

What are our thoughts about muscles? Make use of them or discard them. The same holds for self-assurance!

Now, let's look at some ways we might begin to strengthen our "muscle" of self-confidence. The more it grows, the more assured we will feel that we can not only handle but also steer the course of our lives. Put another way, we have the power to take control of our lives and ensure that we don't always feel like victims of life.

To pick up new behaviours, there are two main methods:

Copy those who have already mastered this skill. Fake it until you make it.

A hopeful outlook for an optimistic life

Overall, our perspective and attitude on life greatly impact how happy we are in our daily lives and how effective we become. A person who thinks things through will become more relaxed, tranquil, and smiling than someone who always sees the negative side of things, lets pressure get to them, and is always frowning.

Not only does your mental condition affect you, but it also affects those around you; in other words, our mental health affects the day we have. You must develop and maintain an inspirational perspective to live a happy and fulfilling life.

There are many ways to develop a more positive perspective and alter how you think about many situations that arise in daily life. It will take a lot of effort to adjust your attitude and avoid spiralling into pessimism, but the new perspective will come naturally in the end. The five primary points to keep in mind when altering your perspective are:

1. Adopt an optimistic outlook and develop your ability to think strongly daily.

It's best to focus on completing each work at hand, envisioning the satisfaction of completing the activity and the wonderful outcome it will bring.

Never give in to doubt, acknowledge that you've taken on a lot, and just keep moving forward. 2. Avoid letting your conversations get off-topic. It may be easy to let someone undermine you during a discussion, especially if they disagree. Avoid being persuaded to revert to your previous behaviours, change your negative speech to positive, and look for the good in everything and every situation.

3. See the good in everyone around you and encourage them to express it. Doing this can inspire an optimistic attitude in your immediate vicinity.

4. Look for the good aspects of everything you do daily. Even though it might be an uphill task that you detest doing and that makes you feel bad, try to find something that can make it into a situation that gets better over time.

5. Never allow yourself to get distracted or duped into going back to your negative mindset. It takes work to alter the way you feel and think, and if you have been depressed about the world and yourself for a long time, it will take a while for your new perspective to stick.

After some time, you'll realise that by gradually shifting from a pessimistic to a positive outlook, you may alter many aspects of your life. You'll notice that your relationships get stronger, your confidence grows, you become more well-known, you feel happier and more certain than before, and you can run the errands you used to detest without being anxious or stressed out. These are just a handful of the areas in which you can develop a more optimistic view of life, improve yourself, and become more inspirational.

The group of abilities known as "people skills" aids individuals in navigating a range of social circumstances. Social intelligence and emotional intelligence are related to it. It indicates that a person can influence others and circumstances and know what constitutes acceptable behaviour. This chapter focuses on collaborating with others and providing guidance on enhancing social skills.

Examine the chart that is above. This offers a framework for thinking about interpersonal relationships. The node of dominance is shown at the top of the circle; those who possess this node enjoy leading, controlling, and manipulating others. Socially dominating people desire other people to follow them; they do not like being mere followers. The friendly-dominant quadrant is on the right. In this kind of engagement, the socially dominant individual will use their kind demeanour to make others feel more at ease and develop a stronger rapport—all the while, in a way, upholding their supremacy. There is friendship at three o'clock to the right. Being able to make others feel comfortable and help them see someone else as a friend is what it means to be friendly.

We reach friendly-submissive, a distinct form of friendship if we continue around the circle. This kind of friendliness is characterised by someone obedient to the demands or desires of others, as opposed to someone focused on controlling one side of the conversation. Someone who is friends with someone else but never asserts their rights in the relationship and lets the other take charge or make decisions for the two of them is an example of this kind of connection.

Untinged by friendliness or antagonism, pure submissiveness is present at 270 degrees. At this point, a person's interaction or control over another person is neutral. Submissive-hostile behaviour is the next in line, where a person exhibits aggressive behaviour while being obedient to the requirements of others. At the other extreme is antagonism, which stands for someone who is hostile and works against establishing a relationship or showing support for another individual.

The final quadrant is hostile-dominant when the individual seeking power in the relationship is not neutral; rather, they want to control and the assurance that the other will submit to their wishes. They act this way without considering the demands of the other, in contrast to friendly-dominant relationships.

None of these will be suitable or improper every time. Each of these orientations has a proper and improper time to be used; the ability to discern what is appropriate in a given circumstance is necessary. If you observe that your relationships are always more dominant than submissive, you might want to try experimenting and finding those partnerships where you can be submissive. Try to establish relationships where you can be more dominant and communicate your needs and wishes if you find yourself in the submissive quadrant all the time.

As you begin your reading adventure, take this book to learn more about the proximal development zone. This is where you are pushing yourself just enough to grow without going overboard or having unrealistic expectations of yourself.

www.ingramcontent.com/pod-product-compliance
Lightning Source LLC
Chambersburg PA
CBHW052147110526
44591CB00012B/1883